AF416333

iPhone 11

Series USER GUIDE

The Complete Manual to Master Your iPhone 11, 11 Pro, 11 Max and iOS 13.

The Handy Apple Guide

Smart Reviewer

© **Copyright 2019 By Smart Reviewer**

All rights reserved.

This document is geared towards providing exact and reliable information with regards to the topic and issue covered. The publication is sold with the idea that the publisher is not required to render accounting, officially permitted, or otherwise, qualified services. If advice is necessary, legal or professional, a practiced individual in the profession should be ordered.

- From a Declaration of Principles which was accepted and approved equally by a Committee of the American Bar Association and a Committee of Publishers and Associations.

In no way is it legal to reproduce, duplicate, or transmit any part of this document in either electronic means or in printed format. Recording of this publication is strictly prohibited and any storage of this document is not allowed unless with written permission from the publisher. All rights reserved.

The information provided herein is stated to be truthful and consistent, in that any liability, in terms of inattention or otherwise, by any usage or abuse of any policies, processes, or directions contained within is the solitary and utter responsibility of the recipient reader. Under no circumstances will any legal responsibility or blame be held against the publisher for any reparation, damages, or monetary loss due to the information herein, either directly or indirectly.

Respective authors own all copyrights not held by the publisher.

The information herein is offered for informational purposes solely, and is universal as so. The presentation of the information is without contract or any type of guarantee assurance.

The trademarks that are used are without any consent, and the publication of the trademark is without permission or backing by the trademark owner. All trademarks and brands within this book are for clarifying purposes only and are the owned by the owners themselves, not affiliated with this document

Table of Contents

Introduction

September 10, 2019 marks a special day. It is because on this day Apple's iPhone 11 made its historic debut. With brilliance in performance and more sophistication in its design. The iPhone 11 is truly a show stopper to its competitors. With advanced technology at an aggressive price tag, the iPhone 11 is something that an Apple fan has always dreamt about. Keeping that in mind, Apple has also addressed the crowd with the arrival of the bigger and better versions of the 11 series. The iPhone 11 Pro and the iPhone 11 Pro Max. Which are quite similar to the X series in terms of design, but they are on a whole different level in terms of performance and features.

As for the pricing,

- Apple **iPhone 11** - 64GB : $699
- Apple **iPhone 11** - 128GB : $749
- Apple **iPhone 11** - 256GB : $849

The iPhone 11 is something quite surreal and not only does it bring more highly advanced technology but it also has a lower introductory cost than the Phone XR cost in 2018. It combines a large 6.1-inch display with the latest version of Corning Gorilla Glass 6 which can survive up to 15 drops from a height of about 1 meter. It also comes with a premium-feeling body, and arrives with six different color options to choose from, these include Product Red, Black, White, Yellow, Purple and Green. Quite an array of colors isn't it?

This year's iPhone steals the show with the two sensors on the rear, the two wide-angle camera lens offer a new level of imaging capabilities. What makes it more unique is the cameras are telephoto and offers f/2.4 for the ultra-wide and f/1.8 for the regular wide sensors. These sensors are 12MP each, and are raised from the rear of the phone in a square glass enclosure - which looks quite stunning.

The new sensors have higher maximum ISO compared to last year's model. As a result, the night mode is the most impressive part of the iPhone 11's imaging quality. Higher ISO allows the sensors to capture pictures by bringing brightness and clarity to impossibly dark scenes. As for the Portrait mode in the iPhone 11, defocusing the background and quick focus system has vastly improved for better photography.

The Bionic A13 inside the iPhone 11 is the most talked about SoC in the market (which is why we have dedicated a separate chapter for it). Another significant internal addition to the new iPhone 11 and 11 Pro is the U1 chip. All the new iPhones have it inside.

This U1 chip uses ultra-wideband technology. A technology that measures how long it takes for short radio pulses to travel between devices, it works out precise locations for your lost items like a phone or a tracking tag. It could even be used to unlock your car! In the iPhone 11 however, with the

U1 chip, you may be able to ping a tag from your phone to help locate the item inside your house.

The design hasn't updated much from the iPhone XR in 2018. The edges of the iPhone 11 still have the same feel as the older iPhone 6, 7 and 8. But in terms of technical advancement, the iPhone 11 offers Wi-Fi 6, has faster cellular with Gigabit LTE and 2x2 MIMO antennas, but does not offer 5G.

In terms of battery performance, the iPhone 11 models have an hour of battery life boost compared to the XR, and the Pros last even longer. Combined with the A13 processor and 4GB of RAM the new iPhone 11 swoops in to handle all your single-tasking work faster and carry out bigger multitasking operations smoothly.

What more can you ask in the new iPhone? Better water resistance, IP68 under IEC standard offering maxing depth of 2 meters under waters up to 30 minutes. Better and wider Selfie cam with the introduction of Slow-Mo selfies. All these at an aggressive price tag of $ 649. Also, if you buy the PRODUCT RED iPhone, then a portion of that sale will directly go the non-profit, Global Fund, to help fight HIV and AIDS. So by buying a red iPhone, you are helping the cause.

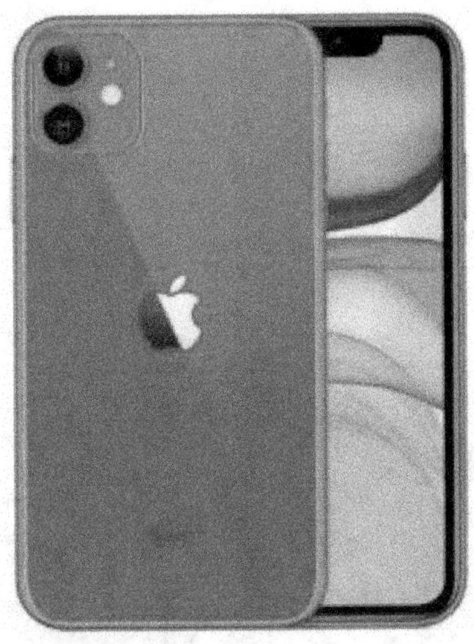

iPhone Product Red. Source Apple.com

Chapter 1

Iphone 11 Processor

Apple's Bionic Chipset has always been ahead of the game. The new iPhone 11 uses an Apple A13 Bionic System-on-a-Chip. This chip also powers the 11 Pro and the 11 Pro Max. But what is it that makes the Bionic A13 stand out to its predecessors? Well, it is most advanced and powerful silicon ever to be used in a Smartphone.

When Apple released the Bionic A12 Chip on their Iphone X series, it was the class-leading chipset which was powerful yet very efficient on the battery life. The A13 Bionic Chipset takes that a notch higher. Not only is this the fastest CPU to ever be created for a Smartphone but it is also the fastest GPU in a Smartphone. But that is not all; while providing more processing power than the A12, the A13 engages in reducing the amount of energy that it requires to handle any calculations. This has allowed Apple to reach significant extra hours of battery life in their new 11 line up, rather than the usual improvements of an hour in their predecessors.

If you are a multi-tasker or a hardcore gamer, then the A13 processor is what you have been looking for. From a light task like browsing the internet to highly CPU intensive work like running multiple apps at the same time, the new A13 flaunts itself in giving you the best experience without any lag in processing. This is only possible due to the highly-efficient 6 cores running on the A13 SoC.

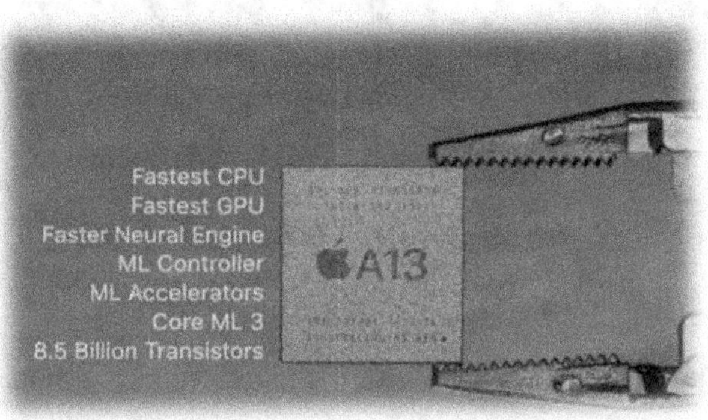

Diving into the technical specifications of the processor, it uses the most advanced 2nd generation 7nm process and consists about 8.5 billion transistors inside it. The cores are divided into two sets, 2 high-performance cores and 4 high-efficiency cores which turn out to be 20% faster than the previous A12. In addition to this, the A13 is capable of performing 1 trillion operations per second making it carry out common machine learning task 6 times faster.

In terms of the GPU, the new A13 is running on 4 cores which is 20% faster than the A12 and 40% more efficient on power consumption. This is why you not only get to experience stunning visuals in games, but also get a few extra hours of gameplay. Also, the Neural Engines run with 8 cores and clocks about 20% faster than the predecessor.

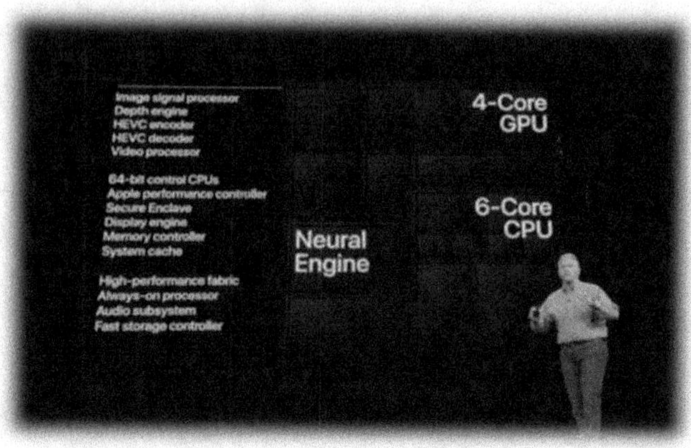

Introduction of A13 Bionic on iPhone 11 Debut

It comes with a Machine Learning Controller, which allows ML models to be scheduled across the CPU, GPU and the Neural Engine, making this a fully integrated platform that can balance efficiency and performance. It can be used for on-device natural language processing, image classification in photos and videos, character animation in AR apps, and a ton more.

Another cool boost up of the A13 Bionic is about how efficient it can run. While the A13 is the most powerful chipset out there, it is also the most advanced chip in terms of power efficiency. The chip uses the second-generation, advanced 7-nanometer process to achieve that level of power management. But it is not just the process and the transistors,

 Apple has optimized the architecture in such a way that by using 4 efficiencies (low-power) CPU cores, you can take on many daily tasks as smooth as butter. Another interesting technique that Apple has done is that it can turn up only specific parts of the chip for a specific task this is done to achieve higher efficiency.

Chapter 2

Iphone 11 Battery At A Glance

Talking about how much juice will you get from the new 11 series? Well, the iPhone 11 Pro and 11 Pro Max are definitely oddities in a way for Apple. The new iPhones are bigger, heavier, and thicker than last year's models. They do not follow the usual slim and light trend by Apple but are more user eccentric in giving their users more hours on the new phones. The run time for the new series can be simply described as four hours better on the smaller phones, and five hours better on the larger one.

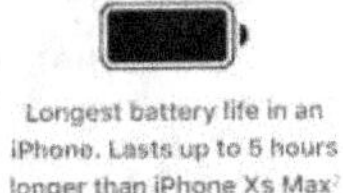

To have a better understanding, Apple has announced the iPhone 11 Pro will last 4 hours longer than the iPhone Xs , the iPhone 11 Pro Max goes up to 5 hours more than the Xs Max and the iPhone 11 gives you an extra hour of usage when compared with the iPhone XR till it runs out of juice. As Apple never unveils the battery capacity in terms of MAh we can only note that these phones definitely surpass the battery life of their predecessors.

For years, people have asked why Apple won't just make phones a little bigger and heavier but offer better battery life. And with the iPhone 11 Pro lineup, it definitely feels that Apple did listen to its fan base.

Chapter 3

Iphone 11 Display

While the iPhone 11 may not have a Super Retina XDR display like its big PRO brothers, it does come with that beautiful Liquid Retina Display straight out of the box. The colors are perfect the view angles are crisp and smooth and come with an HD display. Also, it does have an edge to edge display with slim bezels and come along with the signature iPhone Notch with a front-facing TrueDepth Camera System.

Here is a list of features to dive into about the new display.

- The Apple iPhone 11 sports an identical display to the iPhone XR. You get the same 6.1-inch Liquid Retina screen, which is essentially

Apple's LCD display that is installed on the all major iPhone series like, iPhone 6, 7, 8 but on 11 it is larger in size.

- While the display may not be as sharp as the in comparison to the likes of the 11 Pro, the display of the iPhone 11 will surely satisfy its users. How, you ask? While it doesn't offer mobile HDR compatibility, the iPhone 11 still offers a decent screen with ample brightness and does seem to offer more realistic colors than the Pro models and any other OLED smartphones in the market.

- As for the viewing angles, they are really good and images and text are crisp. In addition to this, iPhone 11 also supports a P3 wide color gamut like the iPhone XR, and also supports features like True Tone technology. True Tone is a feature by Apple which automatically adjusts the display to its surroundings when turned on to create a more refined visual impact.

The display hits 652 nits of brightness when tested and also goes to 113% of the sRGB color gamut. Which is why the display does not deliver oversaturated hues and also brings out rich colors. When compared with the display on the iPhone XR, there does not seem to be any change in both of these devices. The same pixel density of 326 PPI and also the same Pros and Cons of the display in the XR. iPhone 11 does seem to deliver its user the quality of visuals expected by Apple for its price.

Although you may feel like it's a set back with the LCD screen, you also get the advantages of not having to face the issues of an OLED screen, like black smearing and off-axis color shift. Also when its Apple, you do not get the usual LCD, you receive the most advanced LCD Screen available in a smartphone.

Chapter 4

Ios 13 Onboard

Apple announced iOS 13 during the keynote presentation at its 2019 Worldwide Developer Conference on September 11. This is the next version of its mobile operating system iOS 12 which will not only be featured on iPhones, iPads, or iPods near you soon, but will also arrive on the new set of iPhones, including the iPhone 11, iPhone 11 Pro, and iPhone 11 Pro Max. So what is new about the new iOS13 ?, Well, following are the new features you need to know about iOS 13:

4.1 Dark Mode In Ios 13:

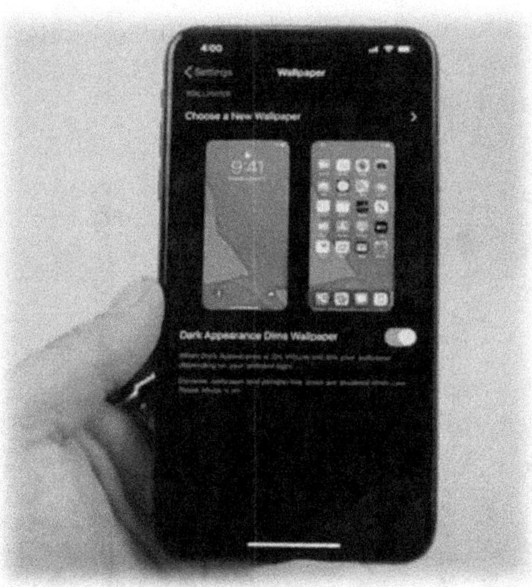

Dark Mode has been arguably the most-requested addition to iOS, and with iOS 13 it finally arrives. The way Apple has executed its Dark Mode on the iPhone and the iPad is quite similar to the execution of the macOS Mojave by the company.

Yes, it makes the general UI a frosty grey and gives all Apple's first-party apps black backgrounds, but it can also be scheduled to only activate after sunset, or during a custom schedule you decide. This feature is also accompanied by four pairs of new abstract-looking wallpapers with light and dark flavours, and the system knows to switch between them depending on which theme is active.

It's all very slick and well thought out, but otherwise, there isn't really much to say about it. There's been a deafening clamour over the last few years to Dark Mode "all the things" in software — a desire that isn't without practical merit, as devices like the iPhone XS which have an OLED display can hugely benefit from the reduced battery consumption as the pixels won't need to generate the white background over and over again.

4.2 Photos In Ios 13:

Apple is making it easier to browse through your photo collection by organizing them down into years, months, and days. When you open the Photos app in iOS 13, you'll see a new "Photos" tab in the bottom toolbar. Tap on it and you'll see four sections: Years, Months, Days, and All Photos. Apple intelligently selects the best photos from your library. You'll find auto-playing videos and Live Photos as you scroll through. Thankfully, screenshots and downloaded images don't make the cut in this feature. The Year section displays your best photo from the given day across all years in the past, making it a simpler alternative to Time Hop.

When you go to the Edit menu while viewing a photo or video, you'll find a new editor. The redesigned photo editor features a more straightforward Instagram-style interface. Below the image, you'll notice a carousel of editing tools. Select a tool and then use the slider to set the intensity. iOS 13 also adds some new editing tools for adjusting Vibrancies, White Balance, Sharpen, Definition, Noise Reduction, and Vignette. In addition to this, Apple now lets the users of the iPhone set the intensity for filter as they desire.

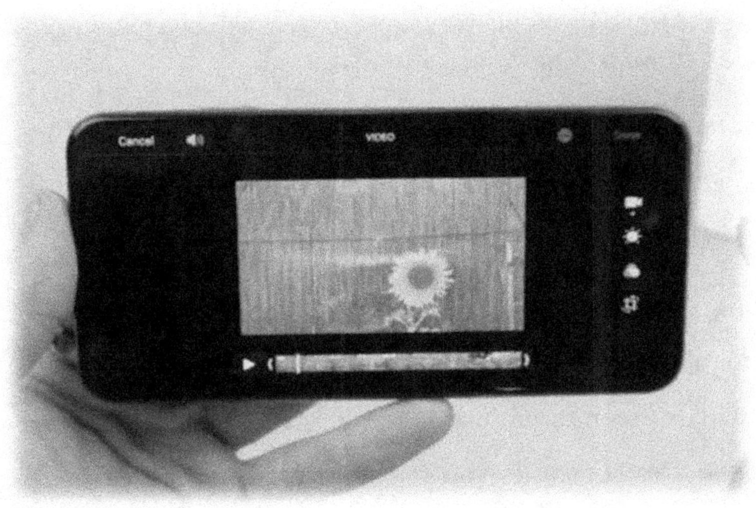

In the new video editor, you can quickly change the aspect ratio, crop, or rotate a video. The video editor also has its own set of adjustment tools which let you increase the exposure and apply filters to your video. All edits for photos and videos are now non-destructive. You can revert to the original media at any given time.

4.3 Maps In Ios 13:

The Maps app gets quite a significant overhaul in iOS 13. Thanks to Apple's new mapping project, the maps data in popular western cities is much improved. Apple will bring the same improvements to more areas around the world as its mapping project progresses.

The Maps app now has a favorites section where you can highlight a place for quick access. You can also use the Collections feature to create a collection of places that you want to visit.

The Maps app also brings its own Google Maps Street View-style feature called Look Around. When you're in a supported location, you can tap on the "Binoculars" icon to jump into the immersive mode. Pan and swipe to move around whichever city you're exploring.

4.4 Reminders In Ios 13:

The new Reminders app looks to be considerably more capable than the original, which was remarkably barebones. For starters, there are now Smart Lists headlining the redesigned interface, which cleverly break your tasks out into groups by what needs doing today, what's scheduled for later and what's flagged as important. And inside your lists, you can even now attach photos, links and documents. Expanded integration with iMessage means that if you tag a contact in a reminder and then message them, that reminder will now pop up as a notification the next time you go to chat. Neat.

4.5 Tighter Location And Bluetooth Access Controls:

Some rogue apps have been using Bluetooth and Wi-Fi data as a workaround for tracking your iPhone's location. In iOS 13, you can now disable Bluetooth access for apps you don't trust. This has nothing to do with using Bluetooth devices for audio playback. Some apps (like Google apps) require Bluetooth access for connecting to accessories like Chromecast.

iOS 13 also revamps the Location Services feature in a big way. An app can no longer get access to constant background location tracking instantly after it's installed. When you first see the popup for location access, the "Always Allow" button won't be available.

Instead, the options are now "Allow While Using App", "Allow Once", and "Don't Allow". "Allow Once" is a new feature that will stop location access once you quit the app (which is great for apps like Uber who are known to exploit this feature).

You can select the "Allow While Using App" to grant location access while using the app. The app can still ping and ask for your location in the background. When it's done that multiple times, you'll see a popup with a map showing how often the app requested your location.

Now you have a choice to either always allow location access in the background or to continue to enable location access only when using the app. You can change this setting at any time by going to Settings > Privacy > Location Services.

4.6 All The Small Things In Ios 13:

It's difficult to note down every little change in the iOS13, even though they have their effect on every bit of the operating system. So to run down the features shortly we have selected only the most important iOS 13 features, such as:

- The **Share Sheet** is the UI element that pops up anytime you opt to share content from your iPhone has now been bolstered with AIsourced suggestions that are dynamic, depending on the app and the individuals you normally share content with.

- The **Health app now supports menstrual tracking**, it is a feature that Apple curiously failed to deliver in previous iterations, forcing users to turn to third-party alternatives instead. The app provides the option to track a wealth of metrics related to your cycle, to help it make more accurate predictions. Now that it's baked into iOS by default, those other apps now stand the risk of being cast aside, a-la the arrival of Screen Time in iOS 12.

- A new accessibility feature, **Voice Control**, allows you to navigate pretty much any aspect of iOS completely hands-free. Voice Control responds to commands to open apps, tap on-screen buttons, enter and edit text and so much more. And if you're using a third-party app like YouTube that doesn't have clearly labelled buttons the system can read, you can say "Show Numbers" or "Show Grid" to select individual UI elements within the screen. I envision a lot of people who don't normally use Accessibility services checking out this one, though those concerned about privacy might be less inclined, as it requires your iPhone to listen to you at all times.

- You can now **swipe to type** on the stock keyboard using the iOS 13's new Quick Path feature, emulating keyboards like Swype and SwiftKey that have been available to Android users for nearly a decade now.

- **New volume and silent mode** graphics make it so the middle of your display won't be obscured when you fiddle with sound while watching a video. Interestingly, the new volume bar, which appears next to the volume buttons in portrait view and at the top of the display in landscape, does collide with some apps' built-in volume graphics that were created to circumvent Apple's design in the first place — YouTube being a notable one. Additionally, when you flip the ring/silent switch, you'll now see a handy alert near the top of the screen.

- **CarPlay now offers a dashboard view** with the ability to show a navigation window in the home screen adjacent to other relevant information, like estimated arrival time and media playback controls. It's actually very reminiscent of Android Auto's old home layout, ironically at a time when Google is simplifying Android Auto's design to more closely imitate CarPlay's classic rows of apps.

- **Memoji can now be sent as stickers**, rather than fully-animated CG models, allowing you to share them with people who don't own iPhones.

- With the addition of **ARKit 3 and Reality Composer**, Apple is making it easier than ever for developers to build apps with augmented reality functions. A new feature, People Occlusion, allow individuals in the camera feed to be placed in the game world.

4.7 Compatibility:

Compatibility on the iOS 13 is definitely not the same as it is on the iOS 12, as most of the things have changed for iOS 13. Apple has also stated that the new iOS 13 will be compatible and available for every iPhone model after the iPhone 6S. This means models like the iPhone 5S, iPhone 6, and also the iPhone SE are most likely to not receive any update for the iOS 13. The elucidation list also includes the 6th-generation and the 7th generation iPod Touch

However, in the scenery for the iPad 2019, it does look like things are about to change. This is because many models will have preinstalled the new iPad OS instead of the iOS 13 to use. Every feature of the iOS 13 will also be included in the iPad OS, also other tablet-specific features are bound to be added in the iPad OS. And as for computability, the new generations iPad OS will be compatible with all iPads after the iPad 2. This means for all the iPad Pro tablets including iPad 5th generation and after and the iPad Mini tablets after the Mini 4.

4.8 Performance In Ios 13:

While Dark Mode and those overhauled apps are nice, though there's one simple change in iOS 13 that could benefit every single facet of the operating system. Apps are now packaged in a more efficient way, making them up to half the size. Updates, on average, are said to be 60% smaller.

Smaller apps translate to more space on your device's storage for other things. But, it also means the apps themselves should open quicker too. Couple that with up to 2x faster app launches in iOS 13 and 30% faster Face ID recognition for devices that support that form of authentication, and it seems Apple's discovered some ways to eke even more speed out of its already-overpowered iPhones.

Apple always manages to find ways to punch up iOS in key areas, but it seems as though they've outdone themselves with iOS 13.

Additions like Voice Control, Sign In with Apple, and menstrual tracking in Health will be extremely valuable to so many people, while the adjustments made to iOS' weaker areas — that confounding volume interface and hard-to-find favourites in Maps — will delight longtime users. Smaller app sizes could also be a game-changer.

Chapter 5

Iphone 11 Vs Iphone 11 Pro Vs Iphone 11 Promax

iPhone Pro , iPhone Pro Max and iPhone 11

When you walk in into an Apple Store, you will be able to check out the new trio on showcase. Although it would be fair to say that the temptations for walking out with a brand new iPhone 11 model are real, you should have an idea about what the models are and how they are different from one another. In terms of size, specifications, and the important issue of price. Here is what you get when you compare the iPhone 11, iPhone 11 pro and iPhone 11 Pro Max.

5.1Starting Off With The Pricing.

Remember the launch of the iPhone XR, how the price gap was kept in terms of the entry-level and the highest featured model. Well, that price gap just got more with the iPhone 11 series.

While the iPhone 11, which is the base variant, starts off at $ 699, The iPhone 11 Pro cost $ 999, which is straight-up $300 more than the base variant and that gap widens up even more when you compare with the iPhone Pro Max which is priced at $1099. Fun fact, the costliest version of the iPhone 11 (i.e. the 512 GB storage version) is still $150 short of the base iPhone 11 Pro model.

5.2 Size And Design

While the iPhone 11 has got itself up to 6 different colour options along with an aluminium glass body, the 11 Pro and 11 Pro Max go for a classier look of 4 matte finished colour option on a stainless steel frame.

All the phones are IP68 dust and waterproof rated and can easily survive up to 2 meters inside water for about 30 minutes. As for the 11 Pro and Pro Max, they can go even deeper, up to 4 meters.

Size and Weight[5]

iPhone 11 Pro	iPhone 11 Pro Max	iPhone 11
Height 144.0 mm (5.67 inches)	**Height** 158.0 mm (6.22 inches)	**Height** 150.9 mm (5.94 inches)
Width 71.4 mm (2.81 inches)	**Width** 77.8 mm (3.06 inches)	**Width** 75.7 mm (2.98 inches)
Depth 8.1 mm (0.32 inches)	**Depth** 8.1 mm (0.32 inches)	**Depth** 8.3 mm (0.33 inches)
Weight 188 grams (6.63 ounces)	**Weight** 226 grams (7.97 ounces)	**Weight** 194 grams (6.84 ounces)

Image credit: Apple

As far as the dimensions go, the new models feature the same dimensions as it was in the iPhone XS, XS Max and XR where the 11 Pro Max tends to be the tallest and widest, having a size of 6.2 x 3.1 x 0.32 inches and also weighing the most at about 225 grams and the iPhone 11 Pro looks to be most compact out of all the variants.

5.3 Switching Over To Display And Battery Life

Apple's Retina display has forever been the most dazzling yet tranquillizing display to be featured in a smartphone. And in the iPhone 11 series, the same tale of two displays for different variants continues.

On the iPhone 11 you will explore the grace of the usual Liquid Retina HD display, while on the Pro and 11 Pro Max, you get to enjoy Apple's Super Retina XDR display. Apple has kept the screen sizes as same last year's phones beginning with the iPhone Pro at a 5.8-inch display, the iPhone 11 with a 6.1-inch display panel and the iPhone 11 Pro Max with a 6.5-inch display. All of these screens feature Haptic Touch on them.

Image credit: Apple

In terms of Battery life, iPhone 11 Pro Max has the highest backup capacity in the entire iPhone lineup to date by lasting for 12 hours of continuous video streaming. Coming right by its side is the 11 Pro which will last you up to 11 hours of web streaming and at last, is the iPhone 11 that can go on for 10 hours of continues streaming playback. While Apple has given fast charging to each of the variants, it's only the 11 Pro and 11 Pro Max that come with an 18-watt charger out of the box. For iPhone 11 however, you do need to buy yourself an 18 Watt Charger since it only comes with the usual 5-watt charger.

5.4 Performance And The Cameras

In terms of performance, all three variants feature the all-new and powerful A13 Bionic Processor. SO there isn't anything much to compare upon the speed as each of the phones are built to give around 20% of a boost to their older models yet being 40% more efficient in power consumption.

As for the Camera, here is where the real differentiation begins.

Image Courtesy TechCrunch

Beginning with the iPhone 11 that is equipped with two rear cameras consisting of a 12 MP wide-angle lens of f/1.8 aperture and another 12 MP ultra-wide lens with f/2.4 aperture. This gives you a 120-degree FOV (field of view) on the wide-angle lens that allows clicking the perfect landscape photo which you always wanted. Whenever you want, wherever you want.

Switching over to the iPhone 11 Pro and the 11 Pro Max, an additional 12 MP telephoto lens with f/2.0 aperture appears to come along both of the wide-angle lenses. The trifecta allows you to click the perfect shot and shoot high-quality 4k videos at 60 fps, on your iPhone.

But when we open the camera in any of the models, all of them supports the same camera features and deliver brilliant pictures.

All of the new phones have the QuickTake feature which allows you to capture still images when you are taking a video. The new Night Mode also delivers amazing low light images. The only difference in feature and photo is when you capture Portrait shots, as the Pro models feature the extra telephoto lens, you do get an advantage while focusing on the subjects for your photo.

Final Verdict

It's without a doubt that the iPhone 11 Pro Max is the clear winner having a bigger screen and a longer battery life than any of the other two. However, you should take note that you will need to pay $1,099 just for its base model. You can save the extra $400 by going with an iPhone 11 as it is much cheaper and gives you the same performance with decent battery life. But if you want to experience a more premium feel at a compact size, the iPhone 11 Pro is for you. Just remember, you are paying $999 for an extra lens and an OLED display.

Chapter 6

Iphone 11 Out Of The Box

The box of the new iPhone 11 looks somewhat similar to the previous iPhone XR box. Here is a quick out of the box showcase of the Green iPhone 11, 128GB model

The box includes the phone itself and along with it comes accessories which include a standard 5-watt charger, we also get wired apple earbuds that have the lightning cable attached, and then we have our USB to lighting cable. Besides all that we also get a quick start guide, a sim card ejector tool, warranty card and apple stickers inside of the box.

Now putting all that aside, looking at the phone, we have got a plastic film on the front side of the iPhone but surprisingly there was no plastic film at the back of the phone.

The back of the iPhone 11 has a glossy sheen but the glass around the camera is not glossy, it is a more matte finish. The phone feels the same way as last year's iPhone XR, size-wise they both are identical and the power and volume buttons are in the same place as well as the silent switch and the displays are the same as well.

Now powering on the phone, we get an Apple logo on booting up corresponding with a greeting message displaying "Hello". The very first thing you'll need to do while setting up the phone is to swipe up from the bottom and select your preferred language, and then select your country or region.

And the next step is to select your Wi-Fi, you do have another option to connect the phone to mac or pc on the bottom of the Wi-Fi screen. After the Wi-Fi is connected it takes a few minutes to activate the phone.

After that, we get data and privacy setup and then we get to set our face id and passcode. In the next step, we get the option to restore a backup from our previous phone or pc. Then we have to login to an Apple ID and then you can either select express settings or the custom settings option.

 After that, you have to accept update services and location services. You also have the option to set up Apple Pay, which you can skip if you want. Then finally we have to set up Siri, Screen time, App analytics, True Tone Display, etc.

Chapter 7

Iphone 11 Initial Setup

So you unpacked your new iPhone 11, but now you need to start setting up your iPhone. How do you do that? Here is a quick and simple illustrative method on how to set up your iPhone 11 from the first boot .

The very first thing you must do while setting up the phone is to swipe up from the bottom and select your preferred language, and then select your country or region.

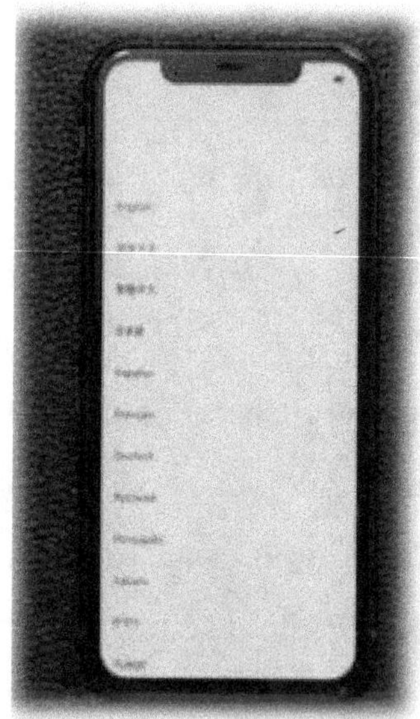

And then a quick start screen comes up, but we can also manually set it up. In this case, we tried to set up manually. In the next step, we need to connect to a Wi-Fi network, you do have another option to connect the phone to mac or pc on the bottom of the Wi-Fi screen as well. After the Wi-Fi is connected it takes a few minutes to activate the phone.

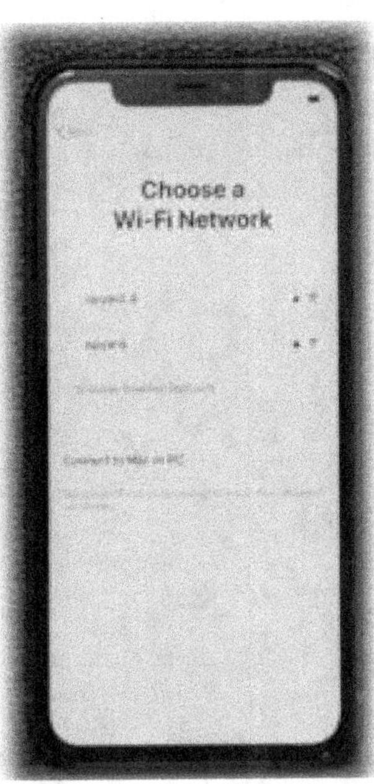

After that we get data and privacy setup and next up we get to set our Face id, you can also skip this to set it up later on.

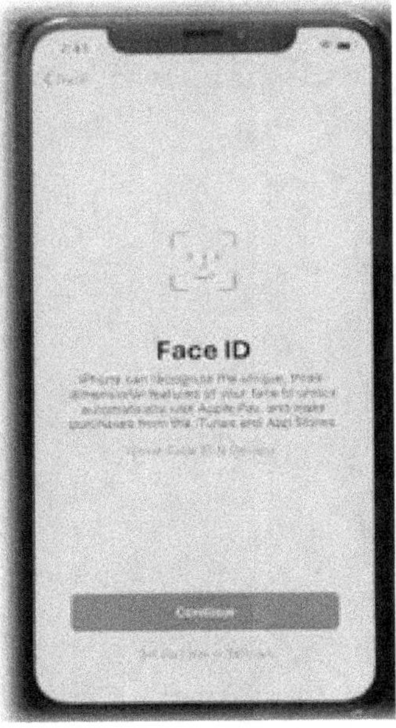

Then we get to set our passcode, after that we get to set our app and data settings.

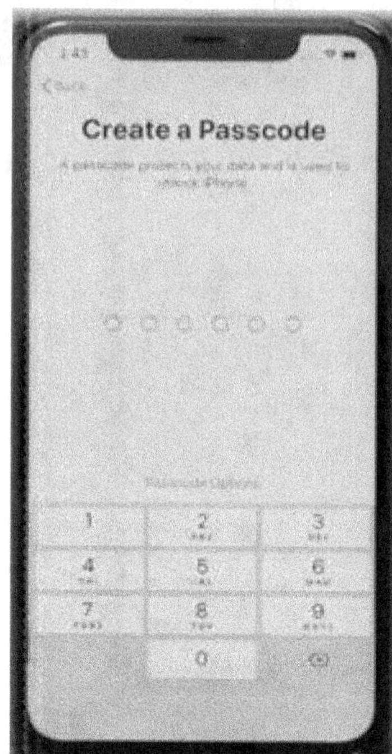 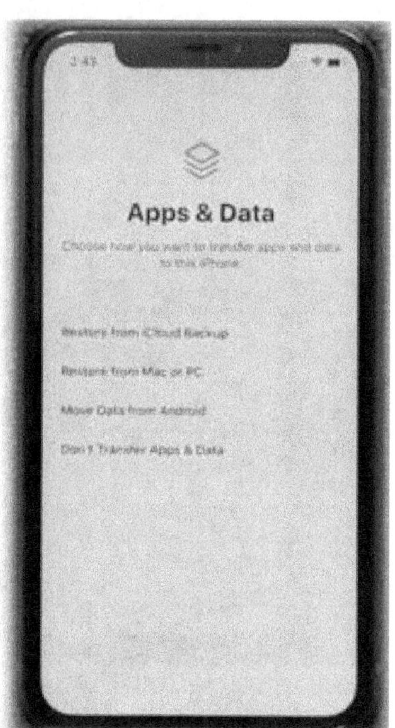

Then it's necessary to log in using an Apple ID, if you don't have an Apple ID you can always set one up. After that we have to accept the terms and conditions, it will take a few seconds for this to process.

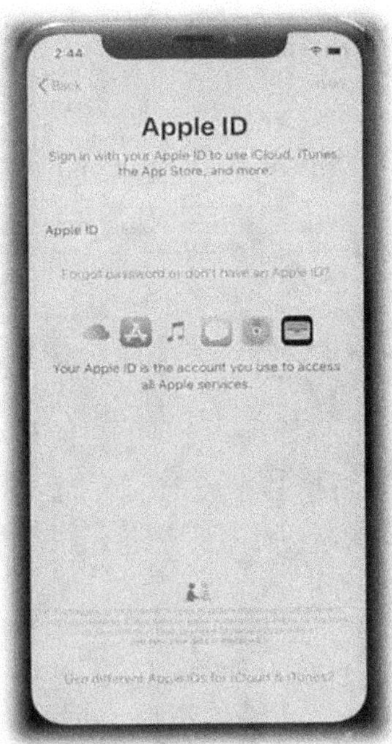

So, after setting up the Apple ID you can continue with the express settings or else you can customize them in terms of iPhone update, location settings, etc.

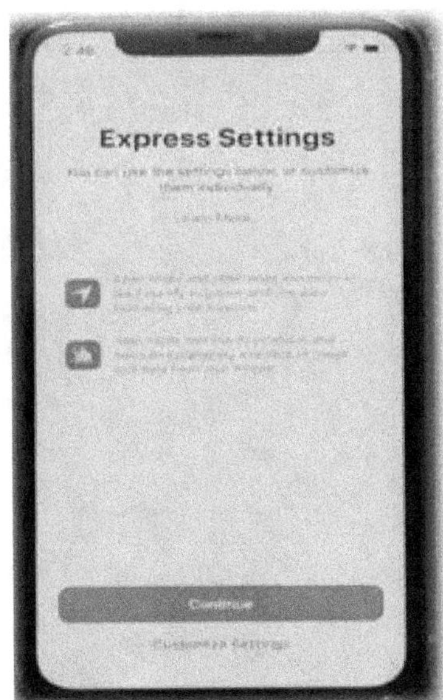

In the customization options, you can setup location settings and Apple Pay.

You also get to set up **Siri** and Screen Time settings.

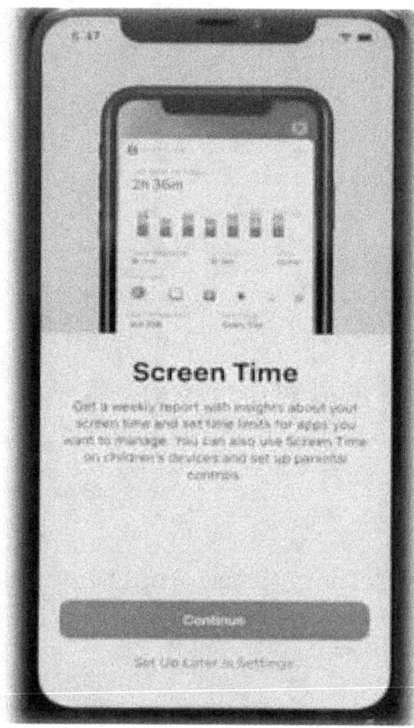

Once you are done setting up all of these, the "Welcome to the iPhone" screen is revealed . You just need to swipe up for the initial setup of iPhone 11 to be completed.

5:49
Welcome to iPhone
Swipe up to get started

Chapter 8

Start-Up Process

Well, the start-up process is similar to the previous generation of iPhones. The only new feature you get in the start-up process is the introduction of being able to choose the DARK appearance mode. Which will be broadly described in further chapters.

Another thing to take notice of is the way of setting up your new iPhone with the data from your previous iPhone. Apple has even simplified the process with iOS 12.4 . No need for the usual iCloud steps. Just a simple new transfer tool is enough to restore your data.

Although it is recommended to use the iCloud backup since it is the fastest way, if you do not want to pay for your cloud storage you can simply just use this transfer feature called Transfer from iPhone, it is available for all iOS systems after 12.4 . We will discuss this system furthermore in another chapter.

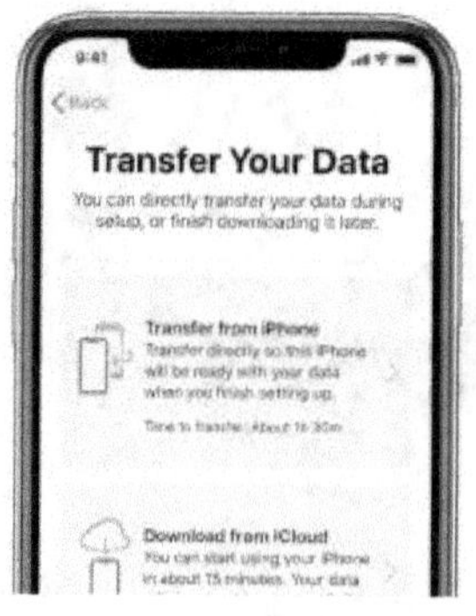

Chapter 9

Battery In Detail

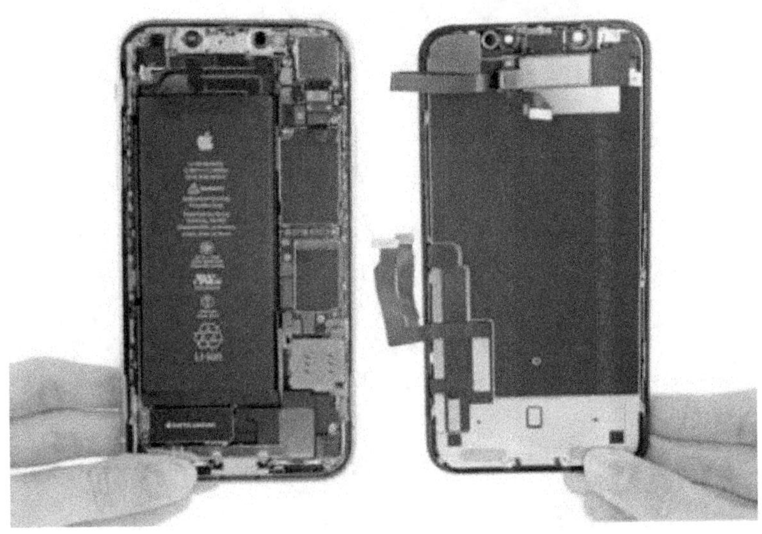

Its isn't just the Bionic A13 that saves the battery life. The juice in the new iPhone 11 series is upgraded in terms of capacity to give a huge boost to battery life. Putting it in perspective of sheer battery life, the last few upgrades for Apple were the iPhone 7 that had around two hours of more battery backup than the 6S and the iPhone X which also provided an extra two hours backup than the iPhone 7. But with the iPhone 11, battery life is a totally different ball game. Apple has offered its best battery life update to date. This gives it about twice the usual extended hours of battery backup.

Diving into details we will find that inside the new iPhone 11 the actual size of the battery has become slightly thicker than before. On paper, it is supposed to last about an hour more than the XR. In terms of playback, it gives around 17 hours, for video, 10 hours for streaming and 65 hours for continuous audio playback. And when tested in the real world situation, the iPhone 11 can easily last a full day at a time.

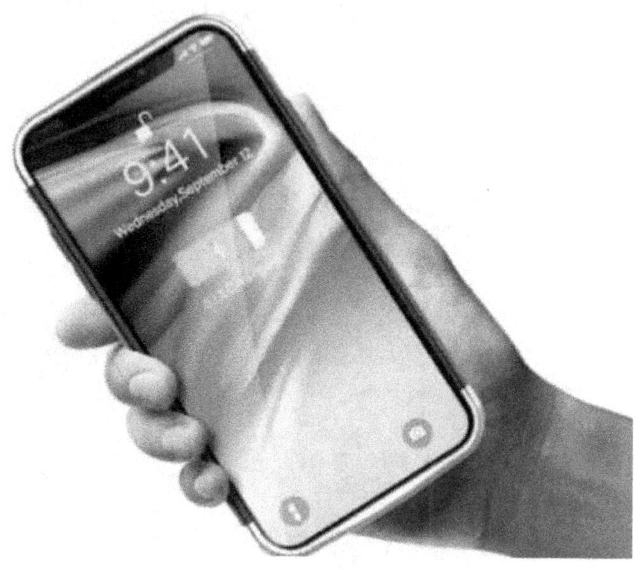

However, if you extensively use the phone, then it is possible that you could manage to kill this battery in less than a day. Which is why the iPhone 11 comes in with Fast Charge support. This jacks up your phone up to 50% in just 30 minutes, provided if you are using an 18W adapter, which is sold separately. (Typical Apple, right?) .

The only downside here is the fact that Apple is still putting its ancient 5W charger in the box for the iPhone 11. So if you want to experience the fast charging experience, you do need to get yourself the Apple 18W charger. Fortunately, for the iPhone 11 Pro, it has an 18W USB-C fast charger.

Finally, in addition to the typical 5W Charger, the iPhone 11 also supports wireless charging, it has a built-in rechargeable lithium-ion battery and also supports charging via USB. Just remember to get yourself an additional 18W charging brick when you walk out with your new iPhone 11.

Chapter 10

Iphone 11 Camera

The biggest standout feature of the Apple iPhone 11 is the camera functionality. There are now two lenses on the rear - normal and ultra-wide - as well as new software-based features like night mode, marking the most significant difference between the 2019 device and the iPhone XR.

The iPhone 11 has dual 12MP ultra-wide (f/2.4) and main (f/1.8) cameras on the back and supports a 12MP TrueDepth front camera. The camera features include Night mode, OIS, portrait mode, portrait lighting (six effects), and also 4K 60fps video recording on both front and rear cameras.

The cameras sit in a raised glass square, but, with just a wide and an ultra-wide lens, the look is a little more subtle. Those two lenses, by the way, are exactly the same as two of the ones on the iPhone 11 Pro. What you lose is a 2X optical zoom .

Apple also updated the TrueDepth camera so it's in line with what you'll find on the Pro models. You can shoot 12 MP selfies and when you switch the phone from portrait to landscape mode, the camera automatically widens its view. There's no wide-angle lens on the front of the iPhone 11. Instead, switching the orientation makes the camera un-crop the frame for a full 12 MP view. You can also force this change to full pixel view by tapping on the double-arrow icon. That same front-facing camera is now also capable of 4K 60 fps video.

In Portrait Mode, the choices have widened to include High-Key Light Mono, a black and white mode that turns the entire background and the gives the user the ability to adjust the highlight with a slider. Apple's done an excellent job with this front-facing camera and the portrait mode algorithm is now much better at capturing photos. In addition, backlight compensation technology is, thanks to Smart HDR, stronger than ever. I'm continually surprised at how much colour accuracy and detail the iPhone 11's cameras can capture even in the harshest backlight.

The camera allows you to also capture 4K 60 FPS video with the rear cameras. In addition, you can combine special features like 240 fps slow motion, panoramas, and time-lapse with the 12MP ultra-wide camera for some eye-pleasing effects.

The most exciting new camera feature is, by far, Night Mode. Apple is late to the night photography game, but I like their approach. The Camera app offers a clear indication of when it's automatically launching Night Mode. You can turn it on by sliding the exposure time to zero.

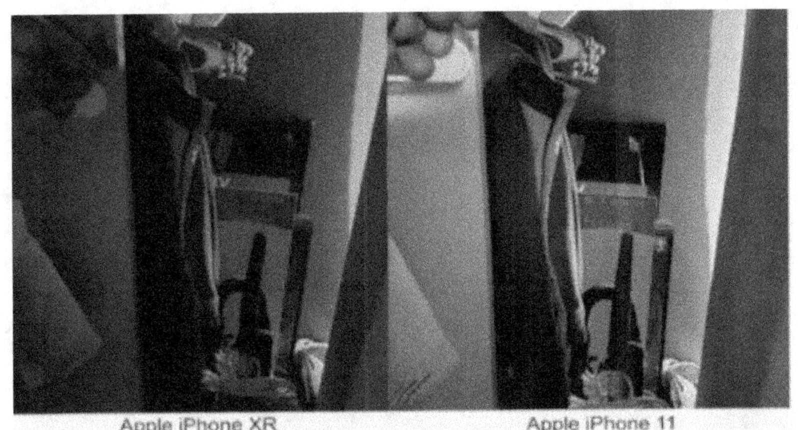

There's a little yellow eclipse in the upper left-hand corner of the camera app screen, this also tells you how long the shutter will be open. When you hit the shutter button, the camera tells you to hold still as it takes the shot. Typical Night Mode shots take between 3 and 5 seconds. However, if you put the iPhone 11 on a tripod, it will happily hold the shutter open for up to 28 seconds. Nighttime star photography is possible with all of the new iPhones.

Chief among them might be the new Camera app, which makes sense since there's so much new photographic capability.

The app has new ways of identifying the three cameras. Ultra-wide is described as 0.5, which I don't really like. You can gesture up from the bottom edge of the image view to open a new drawer with extra features like the timer and HDR controls. In addition, the capture screen will now, in wide camera mode, will always show you how much more of the scene you can bring in with ultra-wide (these image portions appear behind the semi-translucent black bars on either side of the image capture area).

You can now basically switch seamlessly from taking photos to video by holding down the photo button and then, if you want to stay in the video, sliding it to the right.

Videos On Iphone 11

By all means, the new iPhone 11 has redefined mobile photography. How does the iPhone measure up in terms of mobile videography? Here we are going to take a look at the new video capability features on the new iPhone 11.

QuickTake is a brand new feature for the video shooting as this makes it easier to take videos by just long pressing the camera button.

As for the video quality, all iPhone 11 cameras can shoot 4k up to 60 fps for both the front and rear cameras. However it does not come as 4k at 60fps out of the box, you will need to change the video resolutions in settings, how to do that, well just open Settings, then go to Camera then tap Record video and you can select the desired resolution along with the frame rate. So here is storage data of videos per second

- 4k at 24 fps : 135 MB per second

- 4k at 30 fps : 175 MB per second

- 4k at 60 fps : 400 MB per second

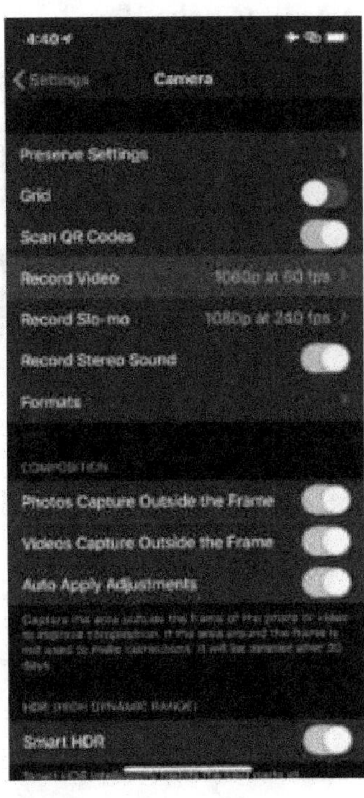
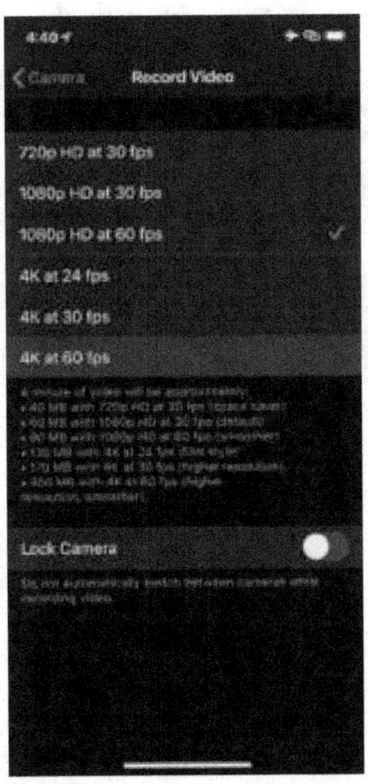

Although that's a lot of storage space which gets eaten up , the lifelike footage which you get at 60fps really totally makes the space to be worth it. The only problem is you cannot choose different resolutions and frame rate for the front and rear cameras, so if you are shooting a low-resolution video from the front and want to shoot a high-resolution video, you need to go back to settings and change that.   But there are third-party apps that you can find on the Apple store which can help you out with this problem. For example, apps like FilMic pro will let you use all of your cameras at once and record from two simultaneously.

 On top of this, you get to enjoy slow-motion video recording of 1080p at 120fps or in Apple's term 'Slofies". Slofies is another new feature for your cameras and you will love to make a lot of TikTok videos using this tool.

As for the TrueDepth system, it is quite similar to the previous iPhone models. Adding in Animojis and it is now used for Face ID.

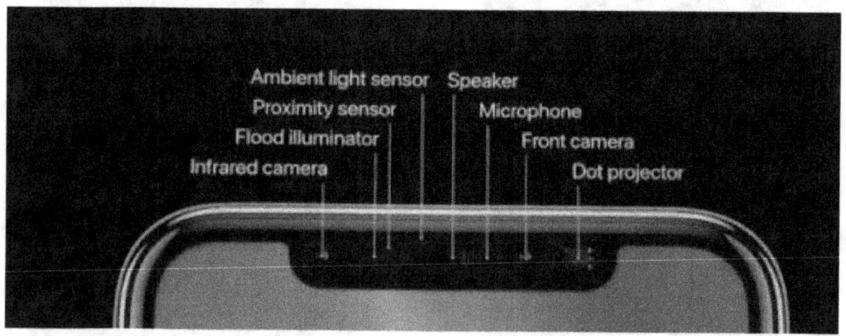

Chapter 11

Setting Up Your Iphone In Details

Setting up your iPhone is not that difficult now, while the initial set up may take up a tad bit of time; It does hold ground being that first and foremost important task. Now we have already discussed in the process of setting up your new iPhone 11 , which includes the first boot-up sequence, setting up face IDs, and eventually making it to the Home Screen with your new Apple ID.

 But what if you already have an Apple ID from your previous iPhone and you want to set up the same setting over to your new iPhone 11. That is what this chapter will cover.

Since the new iPhone 11 has iOS 13. It can only switch user data directly from old iPhones which have iOS 12.4 installed. For the ones who do not have iOS 12.4 in their old models, Apple iCloud Backup is the only available option.

Switching Data From Iphones Without Ios 12.4

This process includes the use of iCloud. You do not need any physical connectors, but fast internet is a must if you want the process to end fast. Here is how you do it.

1. Turn on your new device and place it near your current device that's running iOS below 12.4. Once the Quick Start screen appears on your current device and offers the option of using your Apple ID to set up your new device select Apple ID and then tap Continue. If you don't see the option to continue on your iPhone 11, make sure that Bluetooth is turned on.

2. Wait for an animation to appear on the screen of your iPhone 11. Now hold your old iPhone over the new device and centre the animation in the viewfinder. Wait for a message that says "Finish on the iPhone 11". If you cannot access iPhone 11's camera during the process then select Authenticate Manually, then proceed with the steps that appear.

3. When the dialogue box appears, enter your old device's passcode on to your new device.

4. Follow the instructions and set up Face ID and Touch ID on your new iPhone.

5. A dialogue box will prompt you on your new iPhone to enter your Apple ID password.

6. Then your iPhone 11 will offer you the choice of updating your current device's backup and then restoring or restoring apps, data, and settings from your most recent iCloud backup.

After you select a backup, you can choose whether to transfer some settings related to Siri, Location, Privacy and of course, Apple Pay. Most importantly, do take note that, If you want to update the backup on your device, make sure that Wi-Fi is enabled.

Switching Data From Iphones With Ios 12.4

If your old iPhone and new iPhone 11 are both running on iOS 12.4 or later, you are privileged to have the ability to use iPhone migration to transfer data directly from the phones itself. You even get two options to do the task, either wirelessly, or by connecting the devices together. You may choose the method in accordance with your preferences, whichever you find more swift and hassle-free.

- For migrating data wirelessly, just keep your previous iPhone near your new one throughout the process as you follow the steps mentioned beneath. Also, do make sure to keep both the device connected to power.

- Now to migrate data via a wired connection, you will require the Lightning to USB 3 Camera Adapter and a Lightning to USB

Cable. Firstly, connect Lightning to USB 3 Camera Adapter to your current iPhone, then swoop in the Lightning to USB Cable into your new your iPhone and connect the other end to the adapter.

Now, connect the Lightning to USB 3 Camera Adapter to power through its Lightning port, then follow the steps below.

The Transfer process

1. Turn on your new iPhone and place it near your current iPhone that's running iOS 12.4 or later. If you want to migrate data via a wired connection, connect the devices. The QuickStart screen appears on your current iPhone and offers the option of using your Apple ID to set up your new iPhone. Make sure that it's the Apple ID that you want to use, then tap Continue. If you don't see the option to continue on your current device, make sure that Bluetooth is turned on.

2. Wait for an animation to appear on your new iPhone. Hold your current iPhone over the new iPhone, then centre the animation in the viewfinder. Wait for a message that says "Finish on New iPhone". If you can't use your current iPhone camera, tap Authenticate Manually, then follow the steps that appear.

3. When prompted, enter the password of your old iPhone on your new one.

4. Then set up Face ID or Touch ID on your new iPhone.

5. Tap Transfer from iPhone to begin transferring your data from your previous iPhone to your new iPhone. You may want to check for the transfer icon ⏻ which indicates that your devices are connected.

6. You can also choose to transfer some settings, such as Apple Pay and Siri, from your previous iPhone to your new iPhone.

7. For Apple Watch users, you'll be asked if you'd like to transfer your Apple Watch data and settings.

8. Keep your devices near each other and plugged into power until the iPhone data migration process is complete.
    Transfer times can vary based on factors such as the connection type that you're using, network conditions, and the amount of data being transferred.

Once you are done with the transfer process, there are still some steps left to complete the boot process. All of these steps are discussed below.

Chapter 12

The First Boot

Now that you have backed up and synced your old iPhone setting onto your new iPhone 11, you can start off by booting up your device. Well, the first boot will definitely ask you to go through all the setup processes which we have discussed in the previous chapter. What we are going to discuss now is what you will face after you are done setting up and backing up your required details in your iPhone 11.

So once you are done booting up and setting up the device, what you will notice is a new feature that is choosing the type of theme for your iPhone 11. See an example of this feature below:

What iOS wants here is for you to choose the type of appearance that you require at the moment. As default, the Light Appurtenance will be selected which you can change if you wish by selecting the Dark appearance or by going on to the settings menu.

Now if you select the Light mode, it will be the usual iPhone experience that you have experienced in the previous generations. But if you pick the Dark mode, this will definitely be a new visual delight for your eyes.

By selecting the Dark Appearance mode, you are now allowing iOS to take control of your iPhone theme in a dark black background, meaning all your apps will now give you a different visual experience in this mode.

The main benefit of this mode is for users who use their phone a lot, especially during night time . the new dark mode gives your eyes a much more relaxed and soothing experience while using your phone at night.

After selection is done, just press the continue button and then you will see in the next screen the "Display Zoom" option will come up. What happens here is, you get to choose the type of screen display you want, choosing the Standard will let you have the usual Standard text and controls viewing experience, while selecting the Zoomed mode will magnify that visual input in accordance with your screen.

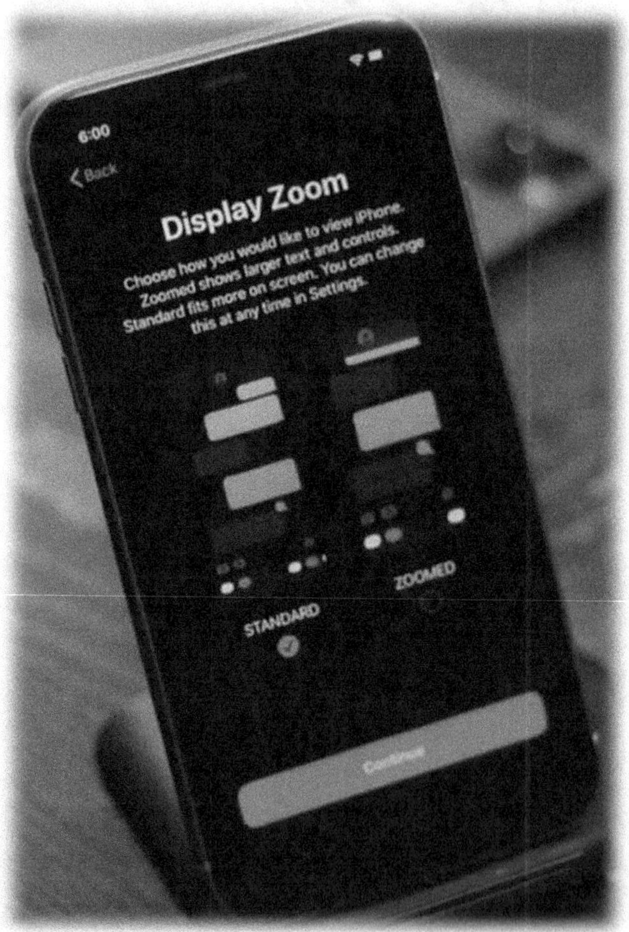

Now that you have selected your preferred screen size option, you just need to press the continue option after reaching the **Go Home** page. The screens will be **Switch Between Recent Apps** and **Quickly Access Controls** Screens

After you finish up these pages, you will set foot into the Welcome to iPhone page. as discussed as earlier, you are just required to swipe up to complete the whole first boot.

So once you are done swiping up, the main Home Screen will appear in front of you and your first boot is thus completed.

Home Screen after the first boot completion.

Chapter 13

Network And Connectivity

Although 5G will not be available in the 11 models, you will definitely get state of the art network models in your iPhone 11.

This includes Apple using Model **A2221*** FDD-LTE (Bands 1, 2, 3, 4, 5, 7, 8, 11, 12, 13, 17, 18, 19, 20, 21, 25, 26, 28, 29, 30, 32, 66). This also supports other network models like the TD-LTE (Bands 34, 38, 39, 40, 41, 42, 46, 48) and even supports UMTS/HSPA+/DC-HSDPA (850, 900,

1700/2100, 1900, 2100 MHz) along with GSM/EDGE (850, 900, 1800, 1900 MHz)

Now for network models, the iPhone 11 comes with Gigabit-class LTE with 2x2 MIMO and LAA, it also includes 802.11ax Wi-Fi 6 with 2x2 MIMO. Bluetooth 5.0 wireless technology, the latest Bluetooth technology, is included with the Ultra Wideband chip for spatial awareness. Also NFC with reader mode is included and it also supports Express Cards with a power reserve.

In accordance with that, the usual built-in GPS/GNSS comes along with the digital compass. Options are available for Wi-Fi and Cellular . Another feature is the iBeacon micro-location feature for the iBeacons.

13. 1 How To Connect To A Network Or Select A Network Mode

Usually, when you insert a sim of your local carrier in your iPhone it shows you the bars of your carrier. Even if your carrier offers features like Volte or Wi-Fi Calling, Apple will usually send an update which can be downloaded. However, if you would like to manually update then make sure your phone is connected to a network and then just do the following:

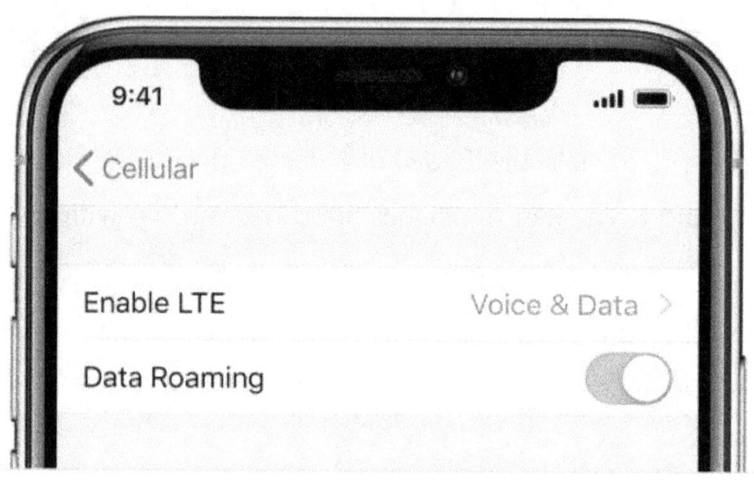

Tap Settings > General > About.

If there is an available update, you will see an option to update your carrier settings. To check your version of carrier settings just browse around the About page and get acquainted with it. For additional carrier details, tap the version number and you can check that out as well.

Activate/Deactivate Mobile Data

For activating or deactivating the mobile data, simply tap on the mobile data icon on the navigation scroll or go to settings and then tap on **Cellular** And then you can choose to activate or deactivate your mobile data.

Roaming Using Your Iphone 11

Data roaming and usual roaming charges do apply on iPhone 11 as described by your cellular carrier service. You do get the option to however choose whether you want to activate the roaming data charges option.

As Your Personal Hotspot

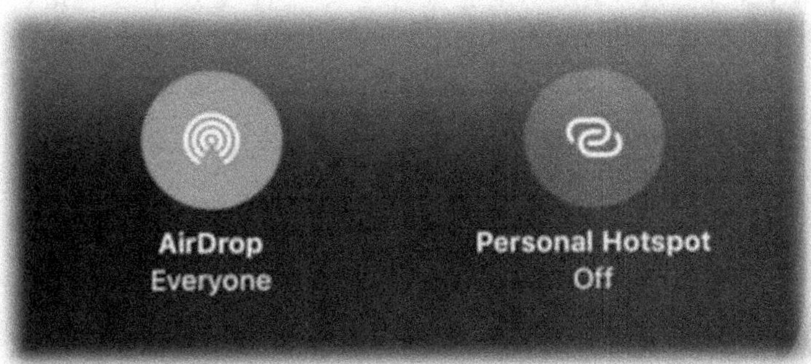

The iPhone 11 can be used as your personal Wi-Fi Hotspot, given your mobile data is on, just tap on to the hotspot icon on the navigation scroll or turn it on by going into your settings.

13.2 Connecting To WLAN (Wi-Fi Or Wireless Network)

Connecting to Wi-Fi is kind of iPhone 101. As when you boot up your phone for the first time, you need to sign in and for that you need to be connected to a Wi-Fi network. Which is quite easy, you can just scroll down the navigation bar and tap on the Wi-Fi icon.

Or you can go on to setting and Turn on Wi-Fi. Your iPhone 11 will automatically search for the available Wi-Fi networks and you can then tap the name of the Wi-Fi network that you want to connect with.

If You Cannot Connect To A Wi-Fi Network

- If iOS detects an issue with your Wi-Fi connection, you might see the Wi-Fi troubleshooting recommendations under the name of the Wi-Fi network that you're connected to. For example, you might see the alert "No Internet Connection." To get more information, tap the Wi-Fi network.

- Try restarting your iOS device, router, and cable or DSL modem. To restart your router or modem, unplug it, then plug it back in. After you restart each device, see if it has fixed the issue.

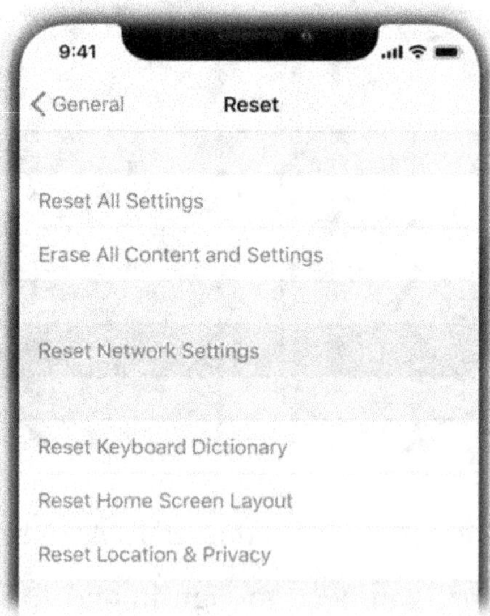

- Reset your Network Settings. Tap Settings > General > Reset > Reset Network Settings. This also resets Wi-Fi networks and passwords, cellular settings, and VPN and APN settings that you've used before.

- Try connecting to a Wi-Fi network in a different location. If your device can connect, you need to get help with your Wi-Fi network. If your device can't connect to any Wi-Fi networks, contact Apple.

13.3 Activate/Deactivate Gps

Here is a simple list on how to set up the GPS on your iPhone 11

1. First up go to Settings ⚙ > Privacy > Location Services.
2. Tap the **Location Services switch** to turn on ⬤ or off ◯ .
3. Tap Share My Location.
4. Tap the **Share My Location switch** for turning on or off.
5. Tap ‹ **Location Services** and return to the previous screen.
6. Tap System Services.

7. Select the desired system service switches.

8. Tap Significant

9. **Then tap Locations**.

   → If you do not see 'Significant Locations,' tap **Frequent Locations**.

10. Select Significant Locations switch to turn on or off.

11. Tap the ‹ **Back arrow** to return to the previous screen.

12. Tap the **Status Bar Icon switch** to turn on or off.

Chapter 14

Iphone 11 Benchaptermarks

As the general specification is required for benchmark testing, the iPhone has the following specs:

- **Display**: 1792 × 828 px
- **Chipset:** Apple A13 Bionic
- Processor Cores: 6
- Processor Frequency: 2660 MHz
- **Memory**: 4096 MB
- **Storage**: 64/128/256 GB
- Camera: 12 MP
- **OS:** iOS 13

After numerous test runs on the iPhone 11 , the scores for Geek Bench 5, Antutu, and many more have been listed below. And it does outperform all its competitors in its segment .

Geekbench5 Score:

The Geek Bench 5 version has been used for these scores. Geekbench 5 scores are calibrated against a baseline score of 1000. Higher scores are better, with double the score indicating double the performance.

As for the scores of iPhone 11, it does shows a high score of 1336 in single-core processing and about 3531 in the multi-core processing test runs.

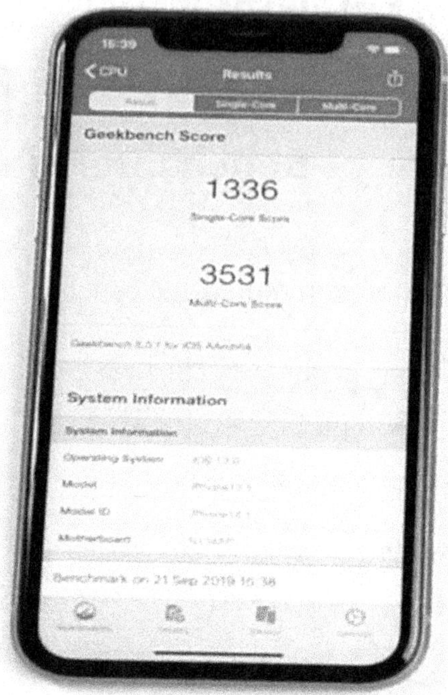

*Please do note that the values may vary slightly during different test runs.

Moving on to the **Metal Test** score, iPhone 11 does score around 6245, with the model being named as iPhone 12. 1 (on Geek Bench 5 it does seem like Geekbench needs to run more beta test on their 5th version).

Antutu Score:

AnTuTu Benchmark is a benchmarking tool used for smartphones and tablets. The use of Antutu is to check the performance of your device. So While running Antutu benchmark on the iPhone 11,

- The CPU score is found to be 147270
- The GPU at about 220278
- The UX score was 77240
- And the MEM score is around 10576

This is quite impressive and it can be considered a very high score when comparing to its competitions.

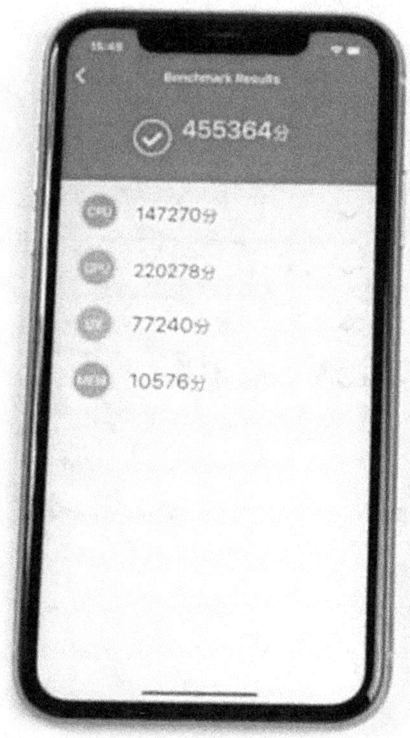

***Please Do Note That The Values May Vary Slightly During Different Test Runs.**

3dmark Slingshot Scores:

3DMark is one of the most famous cross-platform tests and it is used by millions of people. Even the scores on 3Dmark are utilized by hundreds of hardware review sites and many of the world's leading technology companies. So it can be said that it used as a standard benchmark for graphics performance measurement in the industry and also as a professional-grade tool which can be used by anyone for free.

It is comprised of numerous tests to give you the perfect results of your smart phone when compared with other devices. These tests are as follows:

Sling Shot: This is the cross-platform test for the latest smartphones and tablets and 3DMark Slingshot benchmark results comparing mainstream Android and iOS devices. The Sling Shot Tests are divided into four different variants which are:

- Sling Shot
- Sling Shot Extreme
- Sling Shot Extreme Unlimited
- Sling Shot Unlimited

Given below are the results of each test when performed on the iPhone 11.

Performance

Sling Shot Extreme

Score	4902
Physics Score	3248
Graphics score	5742
Graphics test 1	36 FPS
Graphics test 2	19 FPS
Physics test part 1	59 FPS
Physics test part 2	34 FPS
Physics test part 3	16 FPS

Sling Shot Extreme Unlimited

Score	6035
Physics score	3225
Graphics score	8071
Graphics test 1	53 FPS
Graphics test 2	26 FPS
Physics test part 1	80 FPS
Physics test part 2	53 FPS
Physics test part 3	18 FPS

Sling Shot

Score	7048
Physics score	3154
Graphics score	10833
Graphics test 1	99 FPS
Graphics test 2	39 FPS
Physics test part 1	98 FPS
Physics test part 2	53 FPS
Physics test part 3	17 FPS

Sling Shot Unlimited

Score	10306
Physics score	3957
Graphics score	14466
Graphics test 1	187 FPS
Graphics test 2	61 FPS
Physics test part 1	120 FPS
Physics test part 2	44 FPS
Physics test part 3	22 FPS

Ice Storm Scores: Just like Sling Shot, Ice Storm is also a cross-platform benchmarking tool. However, it compares your device with older smartphones and tablets. So 2Dmark Ice Storm is also divided into three different test sections,

- Ice Storm
- Ice Storm Extreme
- Ice Storm Unlimited

Given below are the results of the Ice Storm Test when tested with iPhone 11.

Ice Storm Unlimited

Score	97211
Physics score	33837
Graphics score	209294
Graphics test 1	1044 FPS
Graphics test 2	716 FPS
Physics test	107 FPS

Ice Storm Extreme

Score	MAXED OUT!
Physics score	MAXED OUT!
Graphics score	MAXED OUT!
Graphics test 1	60 FPS
Graphics test 2	60 FPS
Physics test	60 FPS

Ice Storm

Score	MAXED OUT!
Physics score	MAXED OUT!
Graphics score	MAXED OUT!
Graphics test 1	60 FPS
Graphics test 2	60 FPS
Physics test	60 FPS

Chapter 15

Iphone 11 Tips And Tricks

So now you are acquainted with the new iOS13 and can easily use the iPhone 11, but there are some additional features which you may not know. This is because these details do not come on your user manual. So here are a few tips and tricks that will help every iPhone 11 user get the most from their device.

New Gestures available

Users who switched to iPhone 11 from an older iPhone with a home button will definitely need to learn the gestures in order to use their new device fairly easily. Here are a few gestures:

- **Home screen:** Just Swipe up from the Home bar when you are using an app. This will take you back to the Home screen. This gesture also unlocks the device.

- **Notification Center.** Just swipe down from the notch on top of the display.

- **Control Center:** To do this, you will need to swipe down from the top-right side of the display to the right of the notch.

- **Hey Siri :** Now access Siri by just saying "Hey Siri". Quiet convenient.

- **Force apps to quit.** To force stop an app, just Swiping an app card up on the App Switcher.

Enable Dark Mode

To normally switch to Dark Mode you may need to go to Settings . However, this mode can also be turned on by opening the Control Center, tapping and holding on the brightness bar, and then switching Dark Mode by its toggle.

Use Ultra-Wide Camera

Instead of a telephonic lens, the iPhone 11 adds an Ultra-Wide Camera at the back for those wide shots. You can use this new sensor by just Simply tapping on the 0.5x button when using the camera app .

Slofie

"Slofies" are the slo-mo version of the selfie. This is a cool new feature which you get to experience with the new iPhone 11 lineup. Users can do this by using the front camera, swiping over to the Slo-mo option, then recording a slow-motion video.

Use Night Mode

Apple finally added a Night Mode on their iPhone 11 lineup, allowing users to take dramatic stills during nighttime or in dim lighting conditions. This feature automatically turns on when the Camera app detects low-light situations.

A Home Button

Most people will not know about this, but you can create a virtual Home button in the form of AssistiveTouch. This feature can be turned on by going to Settings, then General, then to Accessibility and then AssistiveTouch.

Get Fast Charging

Apple sends an 18W charger with the new iPhone 11 Pro but doesn't send one with the iPhone 11. Those who buy an iPhone 11 will need to spend a bit more to get fast charging.

Chapter 16

Software At A Glance

The new iPhone has manifested the latest versions of all the iOS software from the Apple Store. While the apps might not have any major updates but the bigger and brighter screen set up does create an astounding presence of the sheer scenic beauty of using the apps through its high-quality retina display. We are going to have a look at all the basic software that comes with the iPhone 11 along with the major apps changes on the iOS 13 and we are going to give you the run down of how to use these apps (if you are a new user).

App Store

Let's begin with what changes you get with the new iOS 13.

A New Feature Called Apple Arcade

Apple Arcade is a game subscription service with over 100 amazing new games all with no ads or additional purchases.

This feature requires a single subscription. This allows you to download and play any Apple Arcade game from the App Store. Also, new games will be added regularly. For your suitability.

You can play Apple Arcade games across iPhone, iPad, Mac and Apple TV, and every game is playable offline.

New Language Supports; Arabic And Hebrew

The App Store now supports Arabic and Hebrew languages .

Option to download large apps by cellular

Now you don't need to be connected to WiFi for downloading large apps. You can choose to download apps and games over your cellular connection

Facetime

Here is Apple's very own true video caller, FaceTime, and we are going to have a look on how to use this app on your new iPhone 11.

First up open the FaceTime app, then you can proceed to make a call. To make a FaceTime call to another iPhone, dial the person's regular iPhone number as usual. You can also, tap the FaceTime app and use an email address if you're using FaceTime to call an iPod touch, an iPad, or a Mac.

If you did start out with a regular call and you've broached the subject of going video, you can tap the FaceTime icon. A few seconds later, the other person gets the option to decline or accept the FaceTime invitation by tapping the red button or the green button, respectively. If on a lock screen, the person can slide to answer.

 If the call is accepted, you'll need to wait a few seconds before you can see the other person. As with other calls, the person can also decline with a text message or ask to be reminded to get back in touch later.

When someone requests to FaceTime with you, you'll appreciate being able to politely decline a FaceTime call. Cool as it can be to see and be seen, ask yourself if you really want to be seen, say when you just get out of bed or before your morning coffee.

Search for any FaceTime calls you previously made by tapping an entry for that call in recents.

The iPhone knows to take the call straight to video, though of course, the person you're talking to has to accept the invitation each time. You can also start FaceTime by tapping a pal's listings in contacts.

If you want to mute a FaceTime video call, tap the microphone icon with the slash running through it. The caller won't be able to hear you but can continue to see you.

The new iPhone series also comes with the same *animojis* and *emojis* feature just like on the iPhone X series. This allows you to add shapes, filters, arrows, and even text during a FaceTime call. Tap the icon that resembles a star to get going.

Photos

Photos have gotten smarter and more personal, with intelligent new features that help you find. So what are the changes that you will find on the new Photos App?

New Auto-Playing Live Photos and Videos

Throughout the Photos tab, muted Live Photos and videos begin playing as you scroll, bringing your photo library to life

Extended Live Photos playback

When you press and hold to play a Live Photo, Photos will automatically extend the video when you have Live Photos taken within 1.5 seconds of each other.

Contextual transitions

Animations and transitions keep your place in the Photos tab, so you can switch between views — like Days and All Photos — without losing your place.

No more similar shots and clutter

Duplicate photos, screenshots, whiteboard photos, documents and receipts are identified and hidden, so you see only your best shots.

Birthday mode

If you have birthdays assigned to people in your People album, the Photos tab will highlight your photos of them on their birthday.

A New Smart album for Screen recordings

All your new screen recordings are now in one place.

Now it has new Video editing support

Adjustments, filters, and crop tools are available when editing your videos; so you can rotate, increase exposure, or even apply filters to your videos. Video editing supports all video formats captured on iPhone, including video in 4K at 60 fps and slow-motion in 1080p at 240 fps.

Search enhancements

You can combine multiple search terms — like "beach" and "selfies" — without tapping each word in the search.

Image Capture API

The Image Capture API lets you import photos directly into an app when a camera is connected to your iOS device

Updated Auto Adjustment

Straighten, crop, and adjust the perspective of your photos automatically.

How to Access Photos

On your iPhone, iPad, or iPod touch with iOS 10.3 or later, go to Settings > [your name] > iCloud > Photos, then turn on iCloud Photos.

Apple Maps

With iPhone 11 you get to experience a new Map which has been rebuilt from scratch all thanks to the iOS 13. This brand new map has resulted in significantly improved and more realistic details for roads, parks, buildings , etc. So what new stuff do you get to experience? Have a look at this:

New 360 view

Explore where you're going before you get there with an immersive 3D experience that gives you a 360-degree view of a location. Also enjoy smooth and seamless transitions as you navigate your way around

Mapkit

Updates include vector overlays, point-of-interest filtering, camera zoom and pan limits and support for Dark Mode.

 Better CarPlay experience

CarPlay now provides easier route planning, search, and navigation. Even other features like Favourites and Collections are also available in CarPlay.

Favourites

Whether it's home, work, the gym, or your kid's school, create a list of collections of the places you visit often for quick, one-tap navigation.

Eta Sharing

This is a cool new feature which lets you share your estimated time of arrival with family, friends and co-workers. If any delay occurs then your ETA directly updates.

Customer feedback

Apple has redesigned the customer feedback experience making submitting incorrect addresses, business locations or operating hours that much easier

Siri

Siri has always been an integral part of Apple. The AI has developed over the years and has become much more convenient . To access Siri , just go to setting and tick the switch for Listen for "Hey Siri" on the Siri & Search option. So what's new with Siri on the iPhone 11

Siri Intelligence

Siri will now offer personalised suggestions in Apple Podcasts, Safari, and Maps. Siri can even detect reminders in messages and events in third-party apps.

SiriKit for Audio

Siri can now play music, podcasts, audiobooks and radio with third-party apps.

Radio

Ask Siri to tune in to your favourite radio station.

Indian English voice

For all the Indian users out there Siri has a new Indian English voice.

Messages

Message has always been on the iPhones and helps to deliver those important texts for you. To send a message on your iPhone 11

1. Open Messages
2. Tap to start a new message or go to an existing conversation
3. Tap the text field, then type your message
4. Tap to send

Now to talk about what new features can be seen on the Message App

New Share Name and Photo Feature

This new feature allows you to automatically share your name and photo when you start a conversation or when the other person responds in a message. Decide whether you share with everyone, just your contacts or not at all. You can even choose to use an Animoji, image, or monogram for your photo.

Reminders

Just like the Maps app, even the Reminders app has gone through some major changes for the iPhone 11. This includes redesigning the app features to be more powerful and allowing more creative ways to create , keep track, and organize your reminders. Other changes include:

A Quick Toolbar

With the new quick toolbar just above the keyboard, it's easier than ever to add times, dates, locations, flags or even helpful attachments to reminders. All without having to go to another screen.

Enhanced Siri Integration

Now you can type longer, more descriptive sentences. Reminders will automatically understand and provide relevant suggestions. This also includes the suggestion of messages by Siri.

Attachments

Add photos, document scans, and even web links to your reminders to make them more informative and useful.

Subtasks and Grouped Lists

Now there are even more useful ways to organise your reminders. Just drag and drop to add subtasks under a single reminder. You can also group multiple lists together.

Smart Lists

This new feature allows you to keep track of your upcoming reminders with smart lists that automatically organise and display them. See only your reminders scheduled for today, reminders flagged as important, or all your reminders across every list in one place.

Customise List Appearance

Now you get to customise the appearance of your personal or shared iCloud lists, choosing from 12 beautiful colours and 60 expressive symbols.

How to use the App

It's quite simple actually,

- Open the Reminders app
- Tap a reminder, then tap the info button to the right of the reminder
- Turn on Remind me on a day, then tap the date next to Alarm
- Set a date and time for your reminder
- Tap Done

Health

The Health **app** gathers health data from your iPhone, Apple Watch, and **apps** that you already use, so you can view all your progress in one convenient place. To activate the Health app

- Open Health app and go to the "Health Data" tab
- Tap on "Fitness" and enable the three currently functional sections
- Tap back to the "Dashboard" tab in Health app to see the three functions and their respective charts

Now that you have access to the Health App, let us see what new changes lie in the New Health App

Period Tracking and Notifications

The new Track features allow you to access all important data about your menstrual cycle. Log your period, including flow level, symptoms like cramps and headaches, and whether or not you experienced spotting. Furthermore, log key fertility metrics, including basal body temperature and ovulation test results.

It also allows you to predict and receive a notification on when your period is likely to begin and end in each cycle for the next three cycles.

Fertile Window Prediction and Notification

View a prediction for when your fertile window is likely to begin and end in each cycle for the next three cycles.

Also, you get to receive a notification when your fertile window is approaching.

Cycle History and Statistics

View your entire cycle history with glanceable views of each cycle's logged period, symptoms, fertile window, and length. This feature also allows you to view the date of your last menstrual period, your typical period length, your period length variation, your typical cycle length, and your cycle length variation.

New Summary View

A new Summary view dynamically presents the information that matters to you most, including alerts, recent entries from your favourites, highlights, and new features to enable.

Highlights

Using data from apps and devices you use most, you can see automatically generated charts and graphics including comparison bar charts and line graphs.

Easy Search & Browse

Find what you need more easily with a new categorisation of data types and improved search of all health data.

Interactive Charts and Filters

View historical data by hour, day, week, month, or year and filter with overlays including historical average, daily average, latest, range and alerts.

A New Profile Page

Track your personal health in a profile that includes medical ID and connected apps and devices.

Environmental Audio Level

View notifications and the environmental audio levels from the Noise app on Apple Watch, with the decibel levels categorised in two ranges — OK or Loud.

Oral Health

Use the new Oral Health data type to track your toothbrushing time.

Activity Trends

Get a view of your long-term progress with key activity metrics, comparing the last 90 days with the last 365 days. If you're starting to trend down, you'll get personalised coaching to get back on track. See trend data for active calories, exercise minutes, stand hours, stand minutes, distance, flights climbed, workout walk pace, workout run pace, and cardio fitness level measured by VO_2 max.

Mail

Mail has foever been an integral part of the iPhone . To set up mail just follow these steps:

- From the "Home" screen, tap the "Settings" icon
- Tap "**Mail**, Contacts, Calendars"
- Select the account you wish to modify
- Tap "SMTP" under "Outgoing **Mail** Server"
- Tap the primary server
- Enter your new password in the "Password" field

Once you set this up, all your mails will arrive on the mail app. Now on the iPhone11, iOS 13 has made some major changes to the app, let's have a look

A New Format Bar

A convenient new format bar appears above the keyboard when you type text, providing comprehensive formatting and attachment options including the ability to scan, insert a photo or video, add attachments, and insert drawings.

Block Sender

Have all emails from a specified sender blocked and move the messages directly to the trash. Blocking a sender works across all your Apple devices.

Extended Reply Menu

In addition to reply, reply all, forward, and print, the reply menu adds convenient access to notify me of replies, mark as unread, move to junk, move to a different mailbox, and flag options, as well as the new Mute Thread option.

Mute Thread

Easily mute notifications from an overly active email thread across all your Apple devices.

Updated Photo Selector

The new photo selector occupies the lower portion of the screen so you can see your email while choosing the photo.

Updated Address Autocomplete

When adding a recipient to an email, Mail lists email address choices under each recipient.

Safari

Apple's Safari the built-in a web browser for every iPhone, iPad, and iPad. This is the default web browser , so whenever you open up the internet on your iPhone it will open up in Safari. Apple has worked hard on Safari for it to become the best browser for iOS and they have been working on improving it every iOS update. New improvements include:

An Improved Start Page in Safari.

An updated start page features Siri suggestions, favourites, and frequently visited websites so you can quickly get to where you want to go.

The Download Manager

Check the status of a file you're downloading, access downloaded files quickly, and drag and drop them into a file or email you're working on. You can even download files in the background while you get work done.

Photo Upload Resize

Choose to resize your photo to small, medium, large, or actual size before you upload it.

Website View Menu

The new View menu in the Smart Search field gives you quick access to text size controls, Reader View and per-site settings.

Per-Site Settings

Choose to enable camera, microphone, and location access depending on the website you're visiting. You can also decide whether to view a website in it is desktop or mobile version, use Reader View and enable content blockers on a per-site basis.

Page Zoom

Quickly zoom in and out of a website's text.

Save Open Tabs as Bookmarks

Save a set of open tabs to Bookmarks so you can quickly reopen them later.

Jump to Open Tab From Smart Search Field

If you start to type the address of a website that's already open, Safari directs you to the open tab.

iCloud End-to-End Encryption

Your Safari history and open tabs that have synced with iCloud are now protected with end-to-end encryption.

Notes

You can find the Notes app on your home screen. But what changes has the new Notes app been equipped with? Here is a list to run that down for you:

A New Gallery View

Now you can see your notes as visual thumbnails, making it easier than ever to quickly find the note you're looking for. It's especially great for notes with images, sketches or Apple Pencil handwriting.

Shared Folders Option

Collaborate on folders with other people by giving them access to a folder's contents where they can add their own notes, attachments, or subfolders.

More Powerful Search

The new and improved search can visually recognise images inside your notes and can help you find specific text in the items you've scanned, like receipts or bills. In addition, you'll receive single-tap search suggestions.

New Checklist Options

Quickly reorder checklist items using drag and drop, swipe to indent them, or move checked items to the bottom of the list automatically. If you've completed the checklist and want to use it again, you can tap to uncheck all the items and start over.

Folders and Notes Management

Organise your notes by creating folders and nested subfolders and easily manage how they're organised in your folder lists.

View-Only Collaboration

Share notes and entire folders as view-only so you're the only one who can make changes.

The apps you read before had gone through some major changes for the iPhone 11. Now let us dive into the apps which haven't gone through many radical changes.

The Contacts App

The Contacts App one of the core apps on the home screen , it allows you to store the contact details and also syncs and backup your contacts into your cloud account. Here are the changes have been to it:

New Relationship Labels

Hundreds of new, more specific, relationship labels in Contacts help users manage their growing contact lists.

Create Memoji

Create a Memoji for yourself and your other contacts directly inside Contacts.

The Calendar App

Nothing major has been added to the Calendar App. But now the Calendar app on iOS 13 supports adding atachments to events in Calender. You can schedule task and view dates on the Calender App which is also available on the Home Screen.

The Phone App

The Caller App of Every iPhone allows you to dial or receive calls from anyone. With the new iPhone 11, you get a new setting that protects its users from unknown and spam callers.

When the setting is turned on, iOS uses Siri intelligence to allow calls to ring your phone from numbers in Contacts, Mail, and Messages. All other calls are automatically sent to voicemail.

The Files App

Apple has created a more advanced Files app. This App allows you to access, manage, and organise files stored on external drives or file servers directly from the Files app.

Reality Composer

Reality Composer is the new iOS 13 apps for creating AR experiences. This new app is made for iOS developers as it lets you produce augmented reality experiences with no previous 3D experience very quickly and easily

The above apps were the ones which have gone through the major and minor changes on the iOS 13 for the iPhone 11. Other Pre-installed apps include:

Apple TV

Apple's TV app on the iPhone, iPad, or Apple TV has a Library screen so you can find all the movies and TV shows you've already purchased or rented on iTunes. To watch Apple TV by using the iPhone as a remote you need to follow these steps.

1. On Apple TV, open the **Settings app**
2. Select Accounts
3. Select Home Sharing
4. Select Turn on Home Sharing
5. Enter your **Apple ID**
6. Select Continue
7. Enter the **password** associated with your Apple ID
8. Select **Sign In**
9. On your, iPhone open the **Remote app**
10. Tap Set up Home Sharing
11. Enter your **Apple ID**
12. Enter the **password** associated with your Apple ID
13. Tap **Sign In** in the upper right corner of the screen

Calculator

To launch the Calculator app from your Home Screen, you can do one of three things.

1. Find the Calculator app icon on your Home Screen.
2. Open the Search bar by swiping down from the centre of your Home Screen and type in "Calculator"
3. Ask "Hey Siri, open the Calculator app"

Clock

Apple's Clock app for iPhone lets you keep track of what time it is or how long it's been, no matter where you are or what you're doing. It wakes you up and makes sure you don't leave anything in the oven long enough to burn. To access the Clock App, just Tap it on the Home Screen and to Set up an Alarm, just press + sign at the upper-right corner of the clock screen.

Compass

Your iPhone has a built-in magnetometer. So that you can you're your iPhone as a Compass. To access Compass and calibrate it:

1. Launch **Compass** from your Home screen
2. Hold your iPhone flat in your palm and follow the **on-screen instructions** when prompted to calibrate. You'll have to tilt your iPhone to **roll the ball around the on-screen circle**
3. Tap the **compass face** once to lock-in that bearing

Now when you stray from that path, you'll see the beginnings of a red circle inside the compass. Spin around so that your white pointer is pointed back on the bearing of your choice.

Ibooks

The Apple Books app aims to make e-readers a thing of the past by turning your iPhone or iPad into your central hub for reading. So how do you Buy iBooks from the app

1. Open iBooks on your iPhone
2. Tap Featured, Top Charts or Search at the bottom of the app
3. Tap a book
4. Tap the book's pric
5. Tap the blue GET button
6. Tap the blue GET button in the confirmation pop-up

And that pays for your book and you're able to begin reading it.

Itunes U

The iTunes U provides everything an instructor needs to bring the classroom together on and iPhone or iPad. By this app, you can build lessons with apps and your own materials, collect and grade assignments, start class discussions, or talk to students to answer questions and provide feedback.

To access iTunes U , just tap the app button and wait for the app to sync with your iTunes Store

Itunes

iTunes is Apple's media library , media player, and internet radio broadcaster . To access any content on iTunes, it must be purchased from the iTunes Store App of your iPhone and to access iPhone you need to follow these steps.

1. Open the iTunes Store App
2. Scroll to the bottom and tap Sign In
3. Tap Use Existing Apple ID, then enter the Apple ID and password that you use with the iTunes Store
4. Tap Sign In

When you sign in to the iTunes Store, you also automatically sign in to the App Store, Music, Apple Books, and Podcasts apps on your device.

Keynote

Keynote is Apple's office tool. It is the all-in-one app to create, edit, and give stunning presentations straight from your iPhone. Apple's Keynote is the presentation component of their iWork productivity suite of software, and a companion app to Pages for word processing and Numbers for a spreadsheet . To open a presentation on keynote just tap the presentation and it will automatically open up in Keynote.

Wallet

Wallet is an iPhone app that organizes your credit cards, debit cards, coupons, movie tickets, boarding passes, and rewards cards all in one place. The cards, coupons, tickets, and passes saved in the Wallet app can be accessed when you use Apple Pay. Now, how do you set up your wallet?

1. Open Wallet

2. Tap + to the right of "Apple Pay." This heading is at the top of the screen.If you only see "Passes," first swipe down to reveal "Apple Pay."

3. Enter your Apple ID password and tap OK and then tap NEXT

4. Lay your debit or credit card face-up on a flat surface

5. Point your iPhone's camera at your card

6. Wait for your card to scan.

7. Tap Next.

8. Enter your card's expiration date and CVV and tap Next.

9. Tap Agree

10. Tap the card image and Tap Done.

Weather

The Blue icon with a cloud and a sun behind it is the default Weather App of Apple. It is called Weather and it does show you the weather in your area or any area in the world that you want to see.

To configure the Weather settings you just need to open up the app and tap on the three horizontal bars in the lower right corner of the screen. And set the temperature by toggling between Celsius and Fahrenheit.

Conclusion

In closing, we have learned that the new iPhones are groundbreaking and immensely innovative. Well, it might not be in ways that you might expect, but they are still immensely solid and capable phones that improve on their respective predecessors in many meaningful ways.

Should you invest in the new iPhone 11? Well if you are using the XR then you may not find much difference, but if you have an iPhone older than the X series, you should definitely grab one of the 11 series. The performance, the picture quality, the backup, everything you ever wanted from an iPhone is what the iPhone 11 delivers. It will fit your budget, it is equipped with all the flagship technicality of the decade, and you also get to choose your favourite colour.

www.ingramcontent.com/pod-product-compliance
Lightning Source LLC
Chambersburg PA
CBHW071538150726
48000CB00002B/856